W9-AWG-638

MOON

Troll Associates

MOON

by Laurence Santrey

Illustrated by Steven D. Schindler

Troll Associates

Library of Congress Cataloging in Publication Data

Santrey, Laurence.
   Moon.

   Summary: Describes the physical characteristics of
the moon and its relationship to the Earth.
   1. Moon—Juvenile literature. [1. Moon] I. Schindler,
S. D., ill. II. Title.
QB582.S26   1985   523.3   84-8441
ISBN 0-8167-0252-7 (lib. bdg.)
ISBN 0-8167-0253-5 (pbk.)

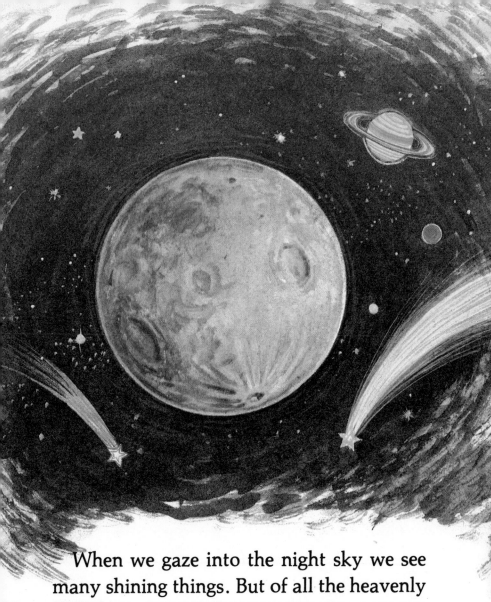

When we gaze into the night sky we see many shining things. But of all the heavenly bodies we can see from Earth, the moon is the closest to us. What is this lovely, silvery ball? It is a great, round mass of rock that never stops circling our planet. The moon is Earth's satellite, its only natural satellite.

There are other "Earth satellites," and each one circles the Earth in its own path, or orbit. But they are not *natural* satellites. They are *artificial* satellites, and they were put into orbit by scientists. They are used for weather forecasting and for television and telephone transmissions. They are just machines, sent up from Earth. Sooner or

later, each one will leave its orbit, fall back toward Earth, and burn up in the atmosphere.

Only the moon never leaves its orbit. Since people first raised their eyes to the sky, the moon has been there. And it will continue to be Earth's constant traveling companion in space.

What is Earth's close companion like? We see it gleam in the darkness, but the moon actually has no light of its own. What shines is sunlight reflecting, or bouncing off, the moon's surface.

The moon is not green with plant life or blue with oceans and rivers. The moon is rocky, dusty, lifeless, and dry. The surface is almost all one color, a dull brown-gray. Much of it is covered with bowl-shaped pits called craters.

Some of the moon's craters are very large—more than 100 miles from one side to the other. Some of the craters are so small that they look as if someone dug out bits of soil with an ice-cream scoop. And there are craters so deep that the tallest skyscrapers would be lost in them.

Around the craters are ridges of rock and dust. The ridges around small craters are not very high. The ridges around the large, deep craters form huge circular walls, like a ring of mountains.

There are also broad, flat plains that look like dark patches on the moon's surface. They were formed by lava that flowed up from below the moon's surface billions of years ago.

Some of the craters on these lava plains look very much like volcanic craters here on Earth. But most of the moon's craters are probably impact craters, formed when huge chunks of space rock—called *meteoroids*—slammed into the moon's surface.

Craters that were formed millions of years ago are still visible on the moon. That's because there is no weather on the moon that can erode, or wear away, its surface. There is no rain, no wind. There is no water and no air.

Because there is no air, the moon gets boiling hot every day and bitterly cold every night. This doesn't happen on Earth because we have an atmosphere of air. The air is like an invisible layer of insulation that keeps our planet from getting too hot or too cold.

The moon does not have an atmosphere

because it does not have enough gravity to keep air from drifting off into space. When astronauts are on the moon, they have to move carefully or they will bounce high up with every step. That's because there is so little gravity pulling them back to the moon's surface.

Even though the moon's gravity is weak, it does have one important effect on the Earth. The pull of the moon's gravity is what causes ocean tides on Earth. Tides are the rise and fall of Earth's oceans.

There are high tides and low tides every day. High tide always takes place on whatever part of Earth is facing the moon. When the Earth turns and another part faces the moon, the area of high tides moves, too.

The moon's gravity is strong enough to pull at Earth's oceans, but Earth's gravity is much stronger than that. Earth's gravity is what keeps the moon in orbit around us. This gravitational pull has to be very strong to keep the faraway moon in orbit.

How far away is the moon? Imagine you are going to circle the world, starting at your home. Now imagine making that trip ten times. When you have finished the tenth trip, you have traveled as far as the distance from Earth to the moon.

Our heavenly companion takes about four weeks to orbit Earth. We call this period of time a lunar month. *Lunar* comes from the Latin word meaning "moon."

In every lunar month there are four phases. In ancient times, people believed that a new moon was born every month.

That is why the first phase is called the *new moon*. When the moon is in its first phase, we cannot see it at all. But we know that in a night or two, a thin slice of silvery moon will appear. Then, as it goes from the first phase to the second phase, we see the thin slice grow thicker.

The new moon continues to grow thicker until, in about a week, we see half of the moon. This is called the *first quarter moon.*

A week after that we see the whole moon beaming like a bright coin in the sky. This is called the *full moon.*

After another week we see about half the moon again. This is called the *last quarter moon.* Every night it grows thinner and thinner until it cannot be seen again. This will be the end of the fourth, or last, phase of the moon.

Sometimes, as the moon circles Earth, it passes directly between Earth and the sun. When this happens, scientists say there is a solar eclipse. *Solar* comes from the Latin word for "sun." During a solar eclipse, we cannot see the sun.

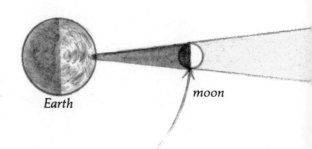

Earth   *moon*

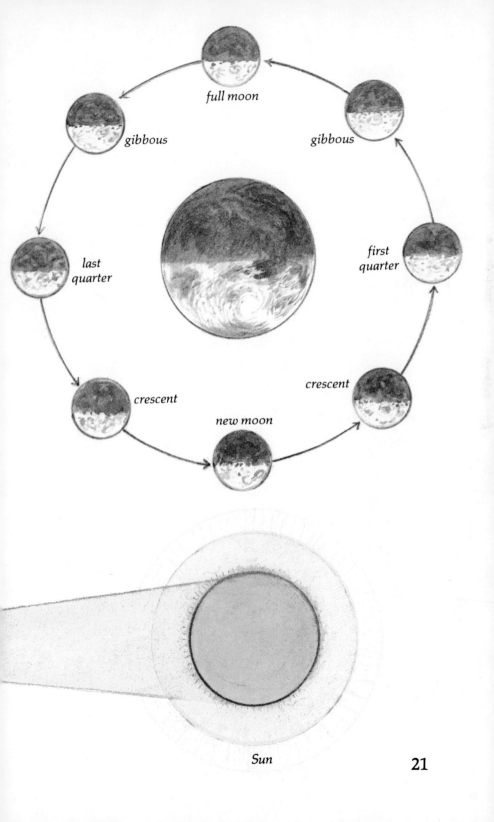

full moon

gibbous

gibbous

last
quarter

first
quarter

crescent

crescent

new moon

Sun

21

There also are times when Earth passes directly between the sun and the moon. When this happens, there is a lunar eclipse. During a lunar eclipse, we cannot see the moon.

Long ago, people were terrified by every eclipse. They thought it was the end of the world, or that the sky gods were angry at them. It seemed a miracle when the eclipse ended.

Throughout history, the moon has been a source of wonder and fascination to people. In many lands, the moon was once worshiped as a god or goddess.

The people didn't understand the reason for the moon's phases, and why the tides always acted in different ways when the moon was new or full or halfway in between. They didn't know about gravity. So they said that the moon god or goddess was pulling at the waters of the world.

Ancient people also kept track of time by watching the moon. The time between one full moon and the next was called a month.

They also saw that, month by month, the sun's position in the sky changed. In the warmest months, the sun rose highest overhead. Then, as it grew cooler, the sun did not rise as high. They saw that it took twelve months for the sun to return to its

highest position overhead. They called this a year. That's how the first calendars came to be.

Not much more was learned about the moon until the invention of the telescope. Using this marvelous instrument, the Italian scientist Galileo studied the mountains and craters of the moon, things nobody had been able to see before.

He studied the dark places—the broad, flat plains—on the moon's surface. They looked like large bodies of water to Galileo, so he called them *maria*, the Latin word for "seas." He gave them such names as the Sea of Tranquility and the Sea of Showers, names that are still used today.

In the centuries since Galileo first studied the moon, we have learned a great many things about our natural satellite. We have learned that there are no seas on the moon. We have learned that there is no water at all on the moon. We have learned how the moon causes Earth's tides.

But not until 1969 did any human being set foot on the moon. Then two astronauts, Neil Armstrong and Edwin Aldrin, made that first incredible journey from Earth to the moon in a spaceship named Apollo 11.

In the three years that followed, there were
five more Apollo missions that landed astronauts on the moon. They conducted many
scientific tests. They collected soil and rock
samples to bring back to Earth. They set up
instruments to measure the moon's heat and
cold, to test for moonquakes and volcanoes,
and to learn more about space, radiation,
and radio signals. They also sent back live

television pictures of the moon's surface and brought back thousands of still photographs.

From these early missions, we have gathered a great deal of information about the moon. But it is just the beginning. One day there may be a space station on the moon where scientists can study the solar system, the sun, and the stars.

Who knows what the future may bring? Someday *you* may take a trip from Earth to our only natural satellite—the moon!